Jobs in
ENVIRONMENTAL
LAW

ROSEN
PUBLISHING®
New York

CHRIS HAYHURST

Published in 2010 by The Rosen Publishing Group, Inc.
29 East 21st Street, New York, NY 10010

Library of Congress Cataloging-in-Publication Data

Hayhurst, Chris.
Jobs in environmental law / Chris Hayhurst. — 1st ed.
      p. cm. — (Green careers)
Includes bibliographical references and index.
ISBN 978-1-4358-3567-2 (library binding)
1. Environmental law — Vocational guidance — United States. I. Title.
KF299.E6H39 2010
344.7304'6023 — dc22

                                                                                    2009025276

Manufactured in Malaysia
CPSIA Compliance Information: Batch #TW10YA: For Further Information contact Rosen Publishing, New York,

New York at 1-800-237-9932

On the cover: This law professor talks to the press outside the U.S. Supreme Court in Washington, D.C.

On the title page: Left: An environmental police officer at work. Right: Two people at work in a law office.

CONTENTS

Introduction

Every society has laws. Recorded by legislators, or lawmakers, laws are intended to maintain order and civility, as well as to ensure justice. Without laws, human society would descend into chaos.

Different kinds of law deal with different subjects. For example, business law delves into the world of corporations, money, and financial transactions. Real estate law covers property sales and homeowners' rights. And then there's environmental law. Environmental law includes all laws pertaining to the natural environment.

Most often, environmental laws are designed to protect the environment from potentially harmful human

intrusions or development. The environment, as a whole, includes the world's forests, rivers, lakes, and oceans. It includes wetlands, deserts, and all kinds of natural open spaces. It includes animals, especially species that are threatened with extinction. It also includes the air we breathe and the water we drink. Environmental law is a tremendously complicated subject, dealing with all aspects of the natural world and the relationship between nature and human society.

There are many fascinating careers available in the field of environmental law. You can pursue a career as an environmental lawyer, a paralegal, an environmental police officer, a legal secretary, or an environmental lobbyist. You could work for a nonprofit organization devoted to protecting wildlife, or you could work for your local government as a water rights specialist. You can work in environmental law enforcement, or you can work in a position where you're the one creating those laws in the first place.

For environmental law to be effective, many professionals must work together in a variety of different roles. Each position requires a unique set of skills and typically attracts people with specialized interests. In the pages that follow, you'll find thorough descriptions of seven jobs in the field. Some of these careers require advanced educational degrees, such as a law degree. Others require more education than high school but less than a four-year degree. And some merely require a high school diploma and on-the-job training. Whatever the case, all of the jobs that follow are within reach of anyone willing to work to get there. Read on to see if a career in environmental law is right for you.

Chapter One

Environmental Lawyer

On television and in the movies, lawyers appear to have well-paying, exciting careers and become famous arguing high-profile cases. However, the truth is that few lawyers (or attorneys) ever see a case that makes major news headlines. And while lawyers make a decent living, few get rich. Most lawyers toil away behind the scenes, their hours spent reading, researching, and writing beneath fluorescent lights in quiet corporate

In 2007, American Electric Power (AEP) and the U.S. Justice Department reached a settlement in a legal case where AEP had been accused of polluting natural areas in the Northeast. AEP paid a $4.6 billion settlement.

offices high above city streets. Others start private practices in small towns, helping the people in their local communities.

So what does an environmental lawyer really do? When it comes to the nuts and bolts of their profession, their job is really not much different from that of any other lawyer.

Being an Environmental Lawyer

Lawyers, including environmental lawyers, work for clients. They represent their clients at trials and do everything they can either to establish their innocence or to prove their opponent's guilt in a court of law. Some lawyers never go to court at all and instead serve as advisers. These lawyers meet with their clients in private and help them make sense of the legal system, including any legal requirements and obligations pertaining to their personal or business lives. Lawyers need to know all current laws and regulations inside and out, especially those that relate to their area of specialization and expertise.

Environmental lawyers specialize in laws pertaining to environmental issues, including water rights, air pollution, land development and preservation, and toxic waste disposal. They may represent and advise individuals, small businesses, major corporations, government agencies, or any number of groups and associations that deal with environmental concerns. They might represent these clients in court, advise them on environmental laws pertaining to their business, and draw up contracts or apply for licenses.

8

Environmental Law in Practice: Desert Justice

Speaking at a career event on the campus of Lewis & Clark Law School in Portland, Oregon, in September 2007, Kristin Ruether, a 2005 graduate of the school, described her job as an environmental lawyer. Ruether worked at the Oregon Natural Desert Association, a nonprofit advocacy watchdog group for the desert country of eastern Oregon. "Most of the issues that we deal with are related to grazing and wilderness," explained Ruether. "Cattle ranching is really big out in eastern Oregon and it's very harmful to the native wildlife of the desert, so we are often challenging projects to increase grazing or maintain grazing that's at a harmful level."

Working in the Private Sector

Environmental lawyers that work in the private sector work for big corporations in major cities, small practices in small towns, and everywhere in between. An environmental lawyer might be part of the staff at a coal mining company, hired to protect the company from lawsuits pertaining to its operations. He or she might represent a real estate firm, hired to ensure that properties located near wetlands, for example, aren't in violation of any environmental laws. Or he or she might work for private garbage-collection companies, brought on to make sure that all aspects of the business adhere to waste disposal laws. When it comes to private sector jobs, it's up to environmental lawyers to help their employers comply with all environmental regulations.

Working in the Public Sector

Environmental lawyers also work in the public sector for major government agencies, like the Environmental Protection Agency (EPA), or much smaller environmental divisions of local governments. Lawyers in public-sector positions are typically hired not only to help governments respect all environmental laws but also to prosecute those who break those laws.

An environmental lawyer at the EPA might spend much of his or her time dealing with Superfund sites. These are "environmental disaster" areas that the EPA has determined are so hazardous, and so in need of remediation, that the federal government has gotten involved in their management and cleanup. An environmental lawyer working for a local municipality, on the other hand, might take on major local polluters. For instance, he or she might deal with a chemical company that is sending wastewater into a river, or a golf course that is using more groundwater for irrigation than the area can support.

Jobs in the Nonprofit Sector

Environmental lawyers in the nonprofit sector work for nonprofit groups devoted to specific environmental causes. They might help a group that fights for better wildlife habitats or one devoted to saving rain forests in South America. They might work for the Sierra Club, Earth Justice, or any of a number of major environmental organizations. They bring lawsuits against individuals and corporations

This lawyer for the Sierra Club speaks to reporters in 2004 after arguing a case in the Supreme Court. The case involved gaining access to government records concerning U.S. energy strategy.

accused of breaking environmental laws. They use the law in whatever way they can to ensure that the special interests of their group are served.

Becoming an Environmental Lawyer: Necessary Skills

If you are smart, enjoy reading and research, have a knack for gathering and organizing information, and like interacting with others, a job as an environmental lawyer might be for you. Of course, having a passion for the environment is also important!

Environmental lawyers, and all lawyers for that matter, must use logic, common sense, and lots of hard work to sort through complicated laws that average citizens find difficult to navigate themselves. It's critical that environmental lawyers have analytical minds. Patience and the ability to remain calm when deadlines are tight is also helpful. Lawyers like to argue. Good lawyers argue their point in clear, concise terms and convince others they are right. If you're a good debater, you might make a good lawyer.

Education and Training

To be an environmental lawyer, you first need to go to college and get a four-year bachelor's degree. After that, you'll have to go to law school. Most law programs take three years to complete and culminate with a degree known as a Juris Doctor (JD) degree. When you finish school, you'll need to pass a written exam known as the

Conducting mock trials, where one person plays a witness and the other plays the attorney, are a great way to learn how cases are tried in court.

bar exam before you can practice law. Individual states have different requirements for new lawyers.

College is one thing. Getting into law school, and getting through it once you're in, is something else altogether. Law school is extremely competitive. A lot of people want to become lawyers, and each year thousands of people are rejected from law schools around the country.

The competition doesn't end with law school, however. Once you graduate, you'll have to fight for a job. Lawyers generally also have to take out loans for college and law school. These loans can be sizeable, and the average law student faces ten of thousands of dollars in student loan debt. There are many more lawyers in the world than there are positions in the job market. Young lawyers have to work hard to find and keep a job.

Starting Out

Most aspiring lawyers begin working as interns while they are still in law school. Even as they shoulder the burden of a heavy course load, they work nights, or whenever they can, at a nearby law firm, nonprofit organization, or government agency. They do thankless jobs like filing, typing transcripts, and researching old cases. They're paid little (if at all) and are often expected to work long hours.

After graduation, it's time to take the bar exam. This is a difficult test that all lawyers must pass in order to practice law. Passing the bar is a big challenge, requiring endless hours of study. It's normal for aspiring lawyers to have to make several attempts to pass the bar.

finding Work as an Environmental Lawyer

Environmental lawyers have to hunt for jobs just like anyone else. Here's an excerpt from an advertisement for a staff attorney posted by the National Environmental Law Center (NELC), which is dedicated to stopping polluters from breaking environmental laws. These are the qualifications that the NELC lists in its advertisement:

> *Candidates should possess initiative, excellent writing and research skills, good judgment, and a commitment to environmental protection. JD required. Candidates for this position should have two to five years of litigation experience. Additional relevant experience, such as political, policy, legal, journalistic, or government experience, is a plus. Advanced degrees in related fields may count toward a candidate's professional experience.*

Note that this position is not an entry-level job. Instead, the NELC is looking for an experienced lawyer who has argued cases in court. If you are seeking a career as an environmental lawyer, you will have to gain experience by spending time working as an intern, and other entry-level positions, before being qualified for a job like this one.

Also note that the employers are interested in other relevant experience that the applicant may have. Because environmental law is a specialized field, any relevant experience that a lawyer might have acquired outside of a school or courtroom, such as working for an environmental nonprofit, may make him or her a more attractive candidate for a particular job. There are many subjects and disciplines that an aspiring environmental lawyer can explore when pursuing a legal career.

Moving Up the Ranks

Once you're working as an environmental lawyer, you'll find that hard work, combined with a bit of good luck, is the key to moving up. Entry-level jobs typically include lots of grunt work: filing briefs, researching old documents, making phone calls, and reviewing judicial records. Entry-level positions are typically designed to bring new lawyers up to speed and to prime them for the more interesting and difficult work ahead.

Thanks to their valuable skills, lawyers, in general, make good money, although just how much depends on where they work. An environmental lawyer working for a public interest group might have a very fulfilling job, but he or she may start out at a lower salary than a lawyer working in the private sector. An entry-level position at a government agency might pay a little more than a job at a public interest group. Those at the top law firms in the United States are paid very high salaries. For up-to-date listings of environmental lawyer salaries, as well as salaries for all other jobs profiled in this book, please check the Bureau of Labor Statistics *Occupational Outlook Handbook*, which is available online.

The Future Outlook for Environmental Lawyers

When it comes to finding jobs, environmental lawyers may have a leg up on attorneys who specialize in different kinds of law. As the population grows, it puts increasing pressure on the environment. More and more species are

Not all of a lawyer's work is conducted inside a courtroom. These lawyers are reviewing evidence for an upcoming trial.

endangered by development, natural resources are threatened by exploitation and overuse, and once-pristine lands increasingly feel the effects of pollution brought on by industrial development. Meanwhile, as people become more aware of the dangers posed by toxins in the environment, by certain agricultural practices, by global warming, or by any number of potentially harmful substances that now exist, there is increasing demand for experts—like environmental lawyers—who can ensure that laws are not broken and justice is served.

Still, especially in times of economic hardship, lawyers are especially vulnerable to layoffs and job loss. When people are pinching pennies, they're hard-pressed to spend big money on expensive lawyers. If you become a lawyer, expect ups and downs. You can make a good living, but there may be times when work is scarce.

Chapter Two
Environmental Paralegal

Paralegals, also known as legal assistants, are most often employed to help lawyers in the day-to-day work that is typical in any law office. While paralegals cannot give legal advice to a client or present a case in court, they can take on many other common tasks that would otherwise be handled by a lawyer.

An environmental paralegal is a paralegal working in the field of environmental law. He or she might assist environmental lawyers, or work for a law firm that handles

Paralegals do important work that can affect the outcome of a trial. This paralegal *(center)* celebrates after helping an attorney win a 2002 court case.

environmental issues. Environmental paralegals might help a lawyer prepare for trial, conduct research on the facts of a case, and identify laws and past legal decisions that might be used in the case at hand. Paralegals organize information, write reports, prepare legal arguments, draft legal documents and motions that are later filed in court, and do many other things that ultimately make an attorney's job easier. Paralegals occupy a special niche in the legal world. They aren't lawyers, but they are extremely knowledgeable about legal matters. Environmental paralegals concentrate specifically on legal issues pertaining to the environment. Many paralegals work for themselves, starting businesses designed to handle nearly all the messy details of any legal case at a much lower cost than typically charged by a law firm.

Working as an Environmental Paralegal

According to the National Federation of Paralegal Associations (NFPA), paralegals that specialize in environmental law perform a variety of tasks. They provide companies with assistance during environmental audits, help companies ensure that all operations are in compliance with applicable environmental laws and regulations, provide legal assistance in situations where environmental violations are suspected, do much of the leg work on environmental issues and laws related to real estate transactions, and keep track of any new laws that might influence the way their clients can operate. Much of the work that paralegals do involves organizing, summarizing, record keeping, and report filing. Paralegals do tons of paperwork, spend a great deal of time sifting through legal documents, and often work very closely with lawyers.

A paralegal employed by a manufacturing company might find him- or herself responsible for keeping the company informed of all rules and regulations that affect the way it does business. He or she might help the company create plans for legal management and hazardous waste disposal, and would certainly be asked to help draft a set of policies and procedures designed to ensure that no employees unknowingly break environmental laws.

A paralegal often works with other professionals in the course of his or her job. For instance, paralegals work with others when helping with environmental audits. Environmental audits are comprehensive examinations of a facility (like a factory, for example) and its affairs, designed to bring to light any environmental violations or environmentally questionable practices that may break the law. Paralegals don't conduct environmental audits themselves. Instead, they help prepare facilities for an audit, take a close look at an audit's findings, organize whatever information is gathered, and pass relevant information on to a lawyer, if necessary.

When lawsuits are filed, a paralegal is employed to do research. Paralegals gather and organize facts and findings, and analyze all of the laws that a legal firm can use in a case. Paralegals essentially do vital grunt work for law firms; they collect evidence, review records, check documents, and create reports. While they don't hold a JD, they do know the law inside and out. Attorneys often look to paralegals for assistance in all aspects of their job.

Skills for the Job

Environmental paralegals have a passion for both environmental issues and the law. They have great organizational skills and are tenacious when it comes to gathering information. They love the legal system and enjoy the prospect of working within it. They recognize how important their job is, and they don't mind the fact that, in most cases, they're paid less and get less acclaim than the lawyers they work with.

If you excel academically, have an interest in law, and don't mind spending much of your time in an office, a career as an environmental paralegal may be for you. To excel as an environmental paralegal, you will need to have the ability to file documents quickly and accurately; the ability to multitask, juggling many assignments at once while never sacrificing attention to detail; the ability to read and summarize legal documents and understand legal terminology; the ability to conduct tedious research; strong computer skills and a working knowledge of many types of software; the ability to work with others as part of a team; good communication skills; and a love for environmental issues like land conservation, pollution remediation, and habitat restoration.

Necessary Education and Training

Formal training is not required to become a paralegal, but it is highly recommended for anyone hoping to land a position in an increasingly competitive job market. The National Federation of Paralegal Associations recommends

Paralegals spend much of their time updating and maintaining files, and working on computers.

that all paralegals have a four-year bachelor's degree, combined with at least twenty-four semester hours of legal coursework.

Paralegal programs are offered at many two- and four-year colleges and universities. Graduates of such programs generally receive a degree or certificate indicating that they've completed formal paralegal training. Most paralegals have an associate's degree or a bachelor's degree. Some even have an advanced (graduate) degree.

Any paralegal that wants to specialize in environmental law should have an environmental background and relevant work experience. An undergraduate degree in environmental studies or ecology, or work experience as a naturalist or botanist, for example, would look great on an environmental paralegal's résumé.

Paralegals with years of experience definitely have an easier time finding new and better-paying jobs than those fresh out of school. Experienced paralegals working at large firms may also have the opportunity to move into management positions. If there's a team of paralegals, somebody has to oversee them all. A senior paralegal is perfectly suited to this job as a paralegal manager.

Getting an Internship

Sometimes it's necessary to have work experience in a law firm even before your first job as a paralegal. The best way to accomplish this is to get a paralegal internship. Most paralegal certification programs now mandate an internship (or two) as part of the educational experience.

Many firms have their own law library where lawyers and paralegals can conduct research and focus on their work.

As an intern, prospective paralegals work under the tutelage of other more experienced paralegals or lawyers.

After completing their internship and working full-time, paralegals can expect to make a decent living, although they will earn less than lawyers. If you work as a paralegal in a big city, for a big law firm, you can expect to make more than a paralegal working for a small firm in a small town. If you have lots of experience in the field, you will probably make significantly more than a paralegal who is just starting out. And if your compensation package includes bonus incentives for productivity, you can

Becoming a Certified Paralegal

Certification as a paralegal is voluntary. Those who choose to become certified often do so for the professional recognition that certification provides.

If you choose to become a certified paralegal, you can do so by taking a test administered by the National Association of Legal Assistants (NALA) Certifying Board for Legal Assistants. The test takes two days to complete, includes five sections, and has questions on communications, ethics, legal research, and legal practice. This might sound simple enough, but it isn't easy to pass the test. In fact, about 60 percent of those who take the test fail their first time taking it!

This is why becoming certified as a paralegal shows potential employers that you know your stuff. Employers may be more likely to hire you as a paralegal if you've demonstrated that you've worked hard to learn the ins and outs of the job, and that you are willing to study hard to become certified. Since paralegals are essential to any law office, competition for these jobs can be tough.

Some paralegals decide to become a member of NALA, which currently represents nearly 20,000 paralegals. Being a member of an organization such as this one may give paralegals an extra edge when it comes to getting a job.

Besides certifying paralegals, NALA also hosts conferences, publishes a paralegal manual and a quarterly journal, holds leadership programs for its members, and administers state-specific advanced competency examinations. For paralegals interested in keeping up with developments in the field, NALA also offers many opportunities for continuing education. NALA is affiliated with dozens of paralegal associations around the United States.

increase your pay by thousands of dollars in any given year. Those with formal training in paralegal work make more money than those without training.

A Secure Career

Environmental paralegals should see their job prospects improve in the near future as environmental issues continue to grow in importance nationwide. The best opportunities will no doubt be for paralegals with formal training combined with an environmental background (a degree in environmental studies, for example).

Paralegals should also see more employment opportunities as they're brought on to handle more and more of the workload once considered strictly the territory of lawyers. When the economy enters a period of recession, people and businesses begin to economize. Lawyers are not immune to bad economic times. When people have less money to spend, they start to question the high fees often charged by legal professionals. They also start wondering what they're getting in return for those fees.

Most lawyers charge by the hour, and most lawyers are very expensive. Clients who are looking to save money search for new ways to cut down on their legal expenses. As a result, some begin hiring paralegals, who offer cheaper rates, to handle their legal needs. Clients sometimes also demand that their lawyers bill by project as opposed to hourly. Or, if a case goes to trial, clients want to pay only if they win.

This can lead to law firms hiring fewer lawyers, paying the lawyers they do hire less, or both. Some law firms lay

Paralegals help lawyers sort through files, legal forms, and other paper-work. Without paralegals, law firms would not be able to function.

off the lawyers they have on staff. Others shut down alto-gether, unable to keep up in difficult economic times. For lawyers, a bad economy is a bad thing. It means fewer jobs and less pay.

Paralegals, however, may not have this problem. For paralegals, a bad economy may sometimes be a good thing. When clients have less money in their pockets, they will often choose a reasonably priced paralegal over an expensive lawyer. This means that paralegals may actu-ally find more work during a recession or economic downturn. In good times and bad, paralegals are seldom left without work.

Chapter Three

Environmental Legal Secretary

Environmental legal secretaries, or administrative assistants, are secretaries that work in legal offices specializing in environmental work. Whether they work for small nonprofits or large private law firms, environmental legal secretaries are a key component of any law office. If your strengths lean toward organization, communication, and the ability to remain calm and focused under intense pressure to meet crucial deadlines, a career as an environmental legal secretary may be for you.

Legal secretaries often work under the direction of an attorney or paralegal. They are an important part of any environmental law office.

Clean Water and the Law

Thanks to a federal law called the Clean Water Act, every person in the United States has a right to clean drinking water. Still, as anyone who's lived in an area with polluted waterways can attest, that right is by no means guaranteed. Industrial chemicals, runoff from agriculture, and countless other pollutants can all find their way into our water supply.

Fortunately for us, there are groups like Lawyers for Clean Water, Inc., a public interest law firm representing environmental groups working to protect the water that every person needs to survive. Clean Water sends its attorneys to the front lines—to the court room, if necessary—in the often-contentious battle between those who rely on a waterway for their drinking supply and those who pollute it. Lawyers for Clean Water, or, for that matter, any environmental law firm, couldn't do their job without the help of skilled legal secretaries. While the lawyers often get all the recognition, it's the secretaries who hold things together behind the scenes.

Providing Administrative Assistance

Secretaries answer phones, type and mail letters, file paperwork, order new office supplies when needed, maintain office equipment, and schedule and plan meetings and conferences. Depending on where they work, a secretary may also be responsible for keeping the office clean and organized, opening up in the morning and closing down at night, and acting as the first point of contact for anyone who walks through the door.

Legal secretaries (including environmental legal secretaries) perform all the same administrative tasks, except that their job is tailored to meet the needs of a law office. They must also type up legal documents such as summonses, motions, complaints, and subpoenas. In addition, they may help out with research from time to time, review legal briefs, and ensure that all documents for a case are ready and in order. Whenever a legal secretary works on a case, he or she does so under the direct supervision of a lawyer or paralegal.

Secretarial Skills

Effective legal secretaries are comfortable around computers, skillful typists, quick readers, and very organized. They are also great with people—always answering the phone, or the door, with a smile. Legal secretaries must enjoy legal work, of course, and environmental legal secretaries certainly should have an interest in environmental issues.

Legal secretaries are often under great pressure to prepare documents quickly and without error. The ability to meet deadlines is critical—to the legal secretary's career and to the law office for which he or she works.

Becoming a Legal Secretary

The baseline requirement for becoming a legal secretary is a high school diploma. However, simply graduating from high school won't set you apart from the competition. It makes sense to consider furthering your education with an advanced degree. If you decide to go to college,

Legal secretaries spend much of their time filing and organizing for upcoming cases.

you could either pursue an associate's degree or a bachelor's degree. You can earn an associate's degree in two years, and a bachelor's degree in four years. It's unlikely that you'll find a major specifically tailored for environmental legal secretaries, but there are many courses that can help prepare you for this career. Taking courses in legal studies, office management, or legal administration would be helpful. Also look for courses that pertain to environmental issues.

Outside of school, the best way to prepare for a career as a legal secretary is to gain hands-on experience working

Secretaries can spend a lot of time on the telephone talking with the people involved in a case.

in an office. Once you land your first job, you'll quickly learn the ins and outs of working in a legal environment.

Future Outlook

The U.S. Bureau of Labor Statistics (BLS) reports that 275,000 individuals worked as legal secretaries in 2006, the most recent year for which data is available. It's unclear how many of these workers were in environmental law.

As is the case with most jobs, the more experience you have as a legal secretary, the more money you can make. Legal secretaries make good salaries, which is one of the reasons why being an environmental legal secretary—as opposed to a secretary in almost any other field—is such a great option.

So what will job prospects be like in the future? That depends on the legal profession as a whole. The BLS predicts the field will grow by around 12 percent by 2016, which means an additional 32,000 jobs will be created. Whatever the case, this fact remains: where there are lawyers and paralegals, there's a need for legal secretaries. And when those legal professionals specialize in environmental law, they hire secretaries who know the terrain.

Chapter Four

Environmental Police Officer

Environmental police officers, also known as environmental conservation officers, are a lot like regular police officers. They wear uniforms, drive official vehicles, and in many cases, carry guns. Environmental police officers typically work for either local, state, or federal governments. However, they usually don't write speeding tickets or make house arrests. Instead, they protect the environment by

This environmental police officer has pulled over a truck that failed its emission test. Environmental police officers spend much of their day in the field, enforcing environmental laws.

upholding environmental laws. Environmental police officers are also called EPOs. Related jobs include environmental conservation officers (ECOs) and wildlife enforcement officers (WEOs).

Environmental Police Officers on the Job

The duties of an environmental police officer vary depending on where he or she works. In general, though, EPOs have the power to enforce any environmental laws, rules, or regulations. They are also obligated to detect and investigate any suspected violations of those laws.

EPOs typically enforce laws protecting fish, wildlife, and plant life; fragile wetlands, streams, and other waterways; vulnerable coastal areas, like sand dunes and tidal estuaries; and parks, reservations, and game preserves. They may also enforce laws pertaining to hazardous waste disposal or storage, air or water pollution, and even littering. If it's a law that has to do with nature or the environment, chances are an EPO knows about it.

Another aspect of many EPO jobs is public education. EPOs will often visit schools, speak at conservation meetings, make presentations at park headquarters, and take part in a variety of other public-outreach events to help educate average citizens about the need for environmental protection.

Finally, EPOs whose jobs include wildlife management responsibilities might be required to check hunting licenses, make sure all harvested game is legal, conduct wildlife surveys, and report on their findings to conservation professionals in other agencies.

EPO Skills

EPOs spend lots of time outdoors, on their feet, in rough conditions, so they need to be in good physical shape. They need to be able to make tough decisions quickly. They also need good people skills, as communicating with the public is a key part of the daily work of any environmental police officer.

EPO jobs also require officers to be familiar with all relevant laws, to understand important environmental issues, and to be physically capable of chasing down and restraining an individual who resists arrest. Many EPOs also carry a gun, so it's also important to know how to safely use a firearm.

To be an EPO, you'll need a driver's license. You may also need a boat operator's license, and you'll probably be required to learn how to drive other vehicles designed to travel over difficult terrain, such as ATVs or snowmobiles. Finally, you'll be subjected to all kinds of tests: medical and psychological assessments, physical testing, and drug testing. Aspiring EPOs must also undergo a thorough background check. This is to ensure that you don't have a criminal record and that you are the type of citizen that the police force can trust.

Becoming an EPO

While there are often no specific educational requirements beyond a high school degree for becoming an environmental police officer, it certainly helps (and is sometimes required) to have an undergraduate degree in

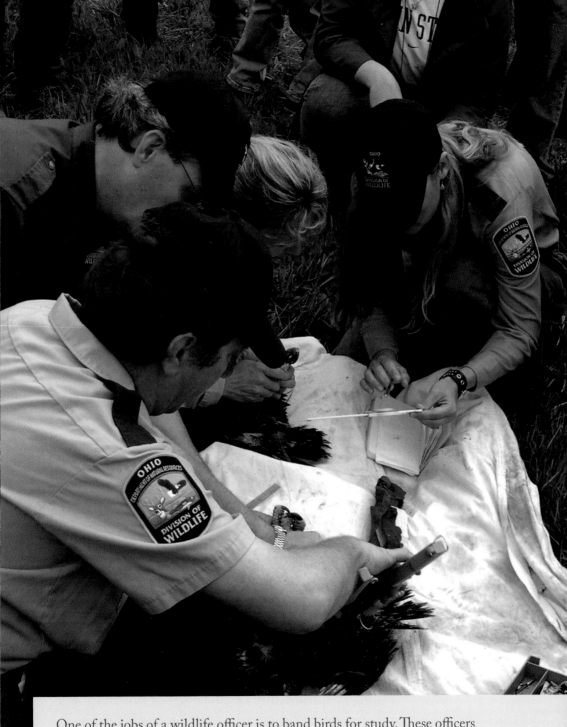

One of the jobs of a wildlife officer is to band birds for study. These officers measure an eaglet's talons before releasing it back into the wild.

a field like biology, natural resources, or ecology. Related work experience is also helpful. Park rangers, conservation professionals, naturalists, wildlife experts, and others with similar backgrounds would all make good EPOs. Many EPOs come to the profession from other areas of law enforcement, bringing skills they learned in their previous work to their new career.

Most EPOs are credentialed by their state following intensive training at a police academy. In some states, that training takes place separate from other police officers, while in others it takes place following successful graduation from the police academy. EPOs are trained and licensed to carry and use firearms, and also receive special training in everything from piloting a boat (for use in patrolling waterways) to wilderness medicine (in the event of an emergency in the field). To be hired on to the police force, they must first pass a battery of exams. After becoming EPOs, they work under the supervision of an experienced officer until they're ready to take on additional responsibilities.

Training and Continuing Education

Throughout their careers, EPOs must continue to prove that they are fit to work. Toward this end, they're required to pass annual physical tests, as well as regular tests of the skills they need to accomplish their job effectively.

Most environmental police officers continue taking classes designed to further their education in enforcement techniques. This annual "in-service" training, designed to keep all officers abreast of new laws, procedures, and environmental issues, is a typical component of most EPO jobs. Such continuing education might last a week or more and typically takes place back at the academy where the officer was first trained. By staying abreast of the latest developments in the field, EPOs ensure that they have the knowledge they need to be effective law enforcement personnel.

Getting Experience

A great way to start off in the field of environmental policing is by getting all the outdoor experience you can. If you like to camp, hike, watch wildlife, or just spend time in nature, you're building on a base of skills, knowledge, and experience you'll need to make your career in protecting those same places.

To Preserve and Protect

In July 2005, thirty-two environmental conservation officers finished their intensive training program at New York State's Joint Training Academy of the Office of Parks, Recreation, and Historic Preservation. At their graduation ceremony, the state's commissioner of the Department of Environmental Conservation, Denise Sheehan, summarized their new job: "Today, New York entrusts these graduates with the preservation and protection of our natural resources . . . Our new ECOs will help ensure the proper protection of our air, water, land, and wildlife through the enforcement of New York State's tough environmental conservation laws and regulations."

Unfortunately, getting into a training program for environmental police officers is highly competitive. A lot of people want this job. If you want to stand out, keep a clean record, do well in school, shadow an EPO on the job if possible, and do lots of work, whether volunteer or paid, related to conservation. Although you may not get paid for some of this work, it will demonstrate that you are interested in environmental issues. Although that may not sound like much now, any experience will look good on a résumé, especially when applying for a job in such a competitive field. By proving that you are willing to work hard early on, you can get a leg up on the competition.

Future Prospects in a Competitive Field

Environmental police officers patrol the boundary between human society and the natural world. As the human population continues to grow, cities become bigger, and suburban sprawl threatens remaining natural areas, the need for EPOs will no doubt increase. The same can be said for EPOs whose main duties include watching out for polluters, wildlife poachers, and the like. Certain people will always try to get the things they want, regardless of the consequences to the natural environment. Environmental police officers are one of the last lines of defense preventing them from doing so.

That being said, there are generally few open EPO positions. Environmental police officers tend to stick with their jobs, meaning that there is very little turnover in the field. As a result, getting work as an EPO can be difficult. EPO

An officer from the Florida Fish and Wildlife Conservation holds a photo showing someone illegally killing a spotted eagle ray.

salaries vary from state to state, and EPOs with more experience or greater responsibilities tend to make more money than EPOs who are just getting started or are still in training.

Chapter Five

Communications Specialist

Communications specialists, also known as public relations specialists, or PR people, are individuals whose job it is to communicate the goals, policies, progress, and developments of the business or organization for which they work.

A communications specialist at an environmental law firm, an environmental nonprofit, or any government

This spokesperson for an environmental organization *(left)* looks at artwork the organization commissioned for a book on endangered animals it is publishing. Spokespersons, PR people, and other communications specialists must be the liaison between their employer and the public.

agency devoted to environmental work or policy would do everything he or she could to "get the word out" on what the outfit was doing. He or she would also be responsible for handling any requests by the public, the media, and others for information about the company or organization.

Working as a Communications Specialist

Communications specialists in environmental law act as middlemen between the company or organization they are working for and the outside world. If you were a communications specialist at a group like the Natural Resources Defense Council, your job might be to tell the media what your group is up to. This can include telling them about lawsuits the Natural Resources Defense Council may have filed, cases that the council won (or lost), and progress made in all aspects of the organization's mission.

Environmental communications specialists often write and distribute press releases, call media outlets like television and radio stations, and send e-mails to their contacts in the outside world. As an environmental communications specialist, you might organize and help run special events designed to raise public awareness, work an information booth at a county fair, or travel far and wide to network with others in the industry. In some positions, you might be responsible for contributing to the company's blog or posting material to the company's Web site. You might assemble multimedia presentations that you or others would deliver, put together fact sheets describing what your organization does and why, and create informational publications for distribution to the public or to the media. You might work with freelance writers, who would help you create content for the company. You might oversee a staff of communications professionals, or you might end up doing everything yourself. It depends on the company or organization you work for.

Being a communications specialist at a private company or at a government agency would involve doing fairly similar work. You would probably participate in many staff meetings and spend plenty of time answering e-mails, writing press releases, and making countless phone calls. A communications specialist does just that: communicates.

Being a Communicator

To be a good PR person at an environmental law firm, environmental advocacy group, or government agency devoted to environmental issues, you need to be a great communicator. When the phone rings and there's a journalist on the other end, you need to know how to give him or her a good quote. You'd also better know exactly what your company is up to and be able to speak about it and write about it in a way that grabs headlines. A communications professional is part cheerleader, part damage-control expert, and part advertiser. You need to be constantly upbeat, able to meet tight deadlines, and willing to take on new projects at a moment's notice. No matter where you work, you'll be the public face for your employer. Make them look good and they'll be happy.

These communications specialists work for the state of Vermont. There are jobs for communications specialists in both the public and private sectors.

Education and Training

Most communications specialists have a degree in communications, journalism, public relations, English, or a similar field. Some have bachelor's degrees, while others go on to get their master's degrees. If you think that you may want to pursue this line of work, it's important to go to college to hone your writing and speaking skills.

A communications specialist in environmental law should complete coursework in environmental studies, ecology, or other environmental subjects, as well as legal affairs, legal writing, and plain old law. Other areas to focus on in school can include science writing, technical writing, environmental journalism, politics and the law, environmental research, public affairs, and public speaking.

When you're in communications, you really need to know what you're talking about. When it's your job to distribute information, you want to get the facts right, be absolutely clear in your message, and always be on target. The right education and training is key. Most public relations pros must have years of experience before they'll be considered for a top position. They'll typically complete an internship during college, gain entry-level experience after graduating, and then go on to move up the ranks.

Career Prospects

The U.S. Bureau of Labor Statistics expects job competition for communications specialists to be stiff in the coming years. It predicts that there will be fewer job openings and many qualified individuals looking for work in this field.

Developing good writing skills is key to being a communications specialist. This graduate student in environmental science journalism joins others in counting birds to get a snapshot of local bird populations.

Despite the fact that this is a competitive field, communications professionals currently in the field will have to retire someday. This will open up positions for new applicants. Overall, the BLS predicts a significant increase in the overall number of communications professionals in the coming years. In addition, a communications specialist interested in environmental law can occupy a special niche within the field. Having a background in environmental matters will give you a leg up when it comes to finding work.

Communications specialists make good money. Salaries vary according to employer. If you work for a private company, you can expect to make more money than you would working for your local government. Working for an environmental nonprofit can mean that, although you may be assisting with very important work, you might make less.

Chapter Six
Environmental Lobbyist

Suits and ties, expensive meals at fancy restaurants, cold-calling government offices, and closed-door meetings with important politicians: it's a day in the life of the professional environmental lobbyist. Lobbyists are government-relations experts. They use their contacts within the political system to influence elected officials to vote in their interest. Environmental lobbyists perform a key role when it comes to getting important environmental legislation passed.

Lobbyists meet at the state capitol in Pierre, South Dakota, to discuss the hundreds of bills being considered by lawmakers.

The Job of an Environmental Lobbyist

An environmental lobbyist lobbies for or against laws that affect the environment. He or she might push for greener building codes, for more public space in an urban area, or for laws that would help organic farmers produce more ecologically friendly food. A lobbyist working for a small nonprofit conservation group devoted to saving wolves in Yellowstone National Park, for example, might lobby state decision makers in Wyoming for stricter hunting laws. A lobbyist working at a group whose mission it is to decrease carbon emissions and reduce global warming might lobby national legislators for policies requiring automakers to make more efficient cars. Environmental lobbyists have the unique ability to directly influence the people in power.

Lobbying itself can take many forms, which are regulated by the law. Lobbyists spend much of their time in an office, sending e-mails, writing letters, and making phone calls. They use networks of friends and acquaintances—their contacts—to gain access to the individuals they want to talk to.

Environmental lobbyists use many techniques to get their message across. Getting "face time" with influential individuals is an important task of an environmental lobbyist. Fishing outings spent chatting about a bill, dinners in exclusive clubs where the intention is to "wine and dine," and numerous other approaches to effectively communicating their needs is the bread and butter of good lobbyists. However, there are strict laws surrounding lobbying practices. For instance, it is against the law for a lobbyist to bribe a politician.

Sometimes lobbyists never reach the person they want to talk to directly but still manage to catch his or her attention. They might get their message on the local news by giving an interview with a reporter, which would allow them to talk about the environmental issue at hand and how their organization feels about it. Lobbyists have to do everything at their disposal to raise awareness about their issue.

Lobbyists are often backed by organizations that have lots of money to spend. These organizations don't mind paying money to a lobbyist that can wield political influence. Successful environmental lobbyists can help get laws passed that can help save the environment.

It Takes a Team

When it comes to environmental lobbying, it goes without saying that the more people you have on your side, the better. Case in point: The Missouri Conservation and Environmental Alliance (MCEA), a coalition of environmental organizations in Missouri that have joined forces to lobby the state's legislators about environmental issues that they feel strongly about. Although the group has not been around for long, it has already achieved a number of concrete victories. For instance, it successfully lobbied lawmakers to pass a "green energy" bill called SB 1181. This bill encourages, and in some cases requires, consumers, businesses, and even the state of Missouri itself to use clean, renewable energy instead of fossil fuels. The MCEA has also stopped bills that would be harmful to Missouri's environment. Thanks to its lobbying efforts, it has successfully been able to advance its agenda of advancing environmental conservation in Missouri.

What It Takes to Be a Lobbyist

Most environmental lobbyists have a bachelor's degree or have completed graduate school. However, no specific degree is required to be an environmental lobbyist. Theoretically, you can become a lobbyist with no degree at all. There is no training specifically tailored for environmental lobbyists, or any lobbyist for that matter. So who's qualified to hold this job?

The answer is, anyone with the skills that will allow them to succeed. Most lobbyists pursue subjects such as history, business, economics, law, and politics in college. These subjects can help them prepare for a career persuading government officials to listen to them. Many prospective environmental lobbyists receive legal training and some attain law degrees. Others have backgrounds in communications or public relations. Many environmental lobbyists have experience working in the U.S. Congress, either as a congressperson, as an aide, or as another type of worker in a congressional office.

Before they'll be considered for employment by a firm representing a specific industry, most lobbyists must gain hands-on experience in that industry. So along with their other qualifications, environmental lobbyists typically have experience doing some type of environmental work as well. For instance, they might start out working at a nonprofit environmental organization.

The biggest skills a lobbyist needs to have are the abilities to listen and communicate effectively, whether it's in writing, over the phone, or in person. A keen understanding of the political process is also important, as is a solid background in law.

This lobbyist for FLP Energy gives the Senate Taxation Committee tapes and other information that detail his company's wind-energy initiatives. He hopes to secure tax breaks for the renewable energy industry that would attract investors.

Successful lobbyists are great talkers and have an uncanny ability to hold people's attention and persuade others to their point of view. A lobbyist who can really get the job done likely has all kinds of political connections. With lots of friends in government, a lobbyist can use those connections in his or her work.

The Rewards of Being a Lobbyist

Since lobbyists come from all kinds of groups with varying financial resources, the average annual salary differs substantially depending on the specific work the lobbyist is doing. Of course, lobbyists for major special interest groups with significant connections in government make huge amounts of money—firms can rake in millions of dollars per year for their lobbying efforts. Top players at those firms make extremely large salaries. Meanwhile, a first-year lobbyist at a small nonprofit that primarily focuses its efforts on state legislation might expect to make much less than the average lobbyist salary. The amount that a lobbyist makes, however, is not necessarily proportional to the impact he or she has in forwarding environmental causes. And while they may not be able to pay huge salaries, many small nonprofits do very important work.

Starting Out

If you think you'd like to be an environmental lobbyist, a great way to start out is as an intern at any level of government. See what lawmakers do and how they interact with the public, and learn all the little details about what makes an official's office tick, and you'll be well on

Some environmental organizations turn to creative solutions when it comes to getting their message across. Here, a "dolphin lobbyist" travels the Metro in Washington, D.C., to raise awareness about legislation that could potentially hurt marine life.

your way to a future in lobbying. You should also gain experience in environmental work. Volunteer with grassroots environmental organizations, and check out the lobbying work to further their cause. If you're lucky, you can help out with their lobbying efforts and gain hands-on experience in the field.

When you're first starting out, any experience is good experience. Internships and other kinds of paid and unpaid work can help give you a solid base of knowledge and skills to build off of. Once you have this on your résumé, you can try for a part- or full-time position either at an environmental lobbying firm or at any organization that is hiring. But beware: competition for these positions is fierce.

Lobbyists often find their first job following a career in government. Elected officials, for example, often become lobbyists once they retire from office. With the access they have to former colleagues, their power and influence can mean big money to the lobbying firm that hires them. A lobbyist with years of successful work under his or her belt might eventually move into a managerial role, overseeing the work of others on the lobbying team. Others might eventually decide to open their own lobbying business. Professional lobbyists who lobby federal officials must be registered to do so, while those who lobby state officials must follow the specific laws on lobbying in that state.

There aren't a lot of lobbying jobs out there, and those that are attract highly qualified individuals. It may take years of experience in government before you'll be considered for a paid position. Those that manage to land a job as an environmental lobbyist can have a very

Lobbyist Steve Wisdom awaits his turn to meet with elected officials. Prior to becoming a lobbyist, Wisdom was the lieutenant governor of Alabama.

rewarding career. Effective and experienced environmental lobbyists will have no shortage of work in the coming years, especially as the country turns more and more toward sustainable and environmentally friendly solutions to problems like natural resource depletion, endangered species, and climate change. That said, grassroots organizations devoted to these causes often have little money to spare and therefore cannot afford to hire large teams of lobbying pros. If you're an environmental lobbyist, you might have trouble finding regular paid work. If you're lucky and demonstrate that you're good at what you do, someone will hire you. Even though it isn't an easy field to break into, with persistence and hard work you can have a career in this field.

Chapter Seven

Environmental Regulations Specialist

When it comes to issues pertaining to the environment, there are so many government-mandated rules, regulations, permits, and guidelines that anyone hoping to stay on top of them all generally needs help. Such an individual, or business, can hire a lawyer who specializes in environmental work. Or they can hire an environmental regulations specialist.

This Tennessee environmental regulations specialist is monitoring the effects that rock harvesting has on the state's waterways. Most environmental regulations specialists spend at least part of their workday outside.

Rules and Regulations

Environmental regulations specialists are individuals who know the rules and regulations of their trade inside and out. An environmental regulations specialist at an oil drilling company would help the company navigate every single law having to do with oil procurement—such as waste disposal, groundwater contamination limits, and what to do in the event of a spill. An environmental regulations specialist at a large logging company might specialize in laws pertaining to logging rights, forest management, and transportation (since shipping the logs to buyers may be part of the business).

Environmental regulations specialists typically have years of experience in the industry. An environmental regulations specialist might have training as an environmental scientist, an environmental engineer, a geologist, or similar profession. He or she would also ideally have government connections and experience, a keen understanding of environmental regulations, and knowledge about what it takes to maintain compliance with those regulations. The environmental regulations specialist's job, each and every day, is to help his or her business stay within the law. He or she may be employed by a private company as a consultant or work on the staff of a company.

On the Job

Environmental regulations specialists research current environmental laws, compile them into an easily referenced document, and keep them on hand for whenever they are needed. They prepare technical reports, organize and

Project/Site: *Mohannah*

Applicant/Owner: _____

Investigator: *WFa)A llied Judson*

Date: *06-11-03*

County: _____

State: _____

Do Normal Circumstances exist on this site?   Yes   No   Community ID: _____

Is the site significantly disturbed (Atypical Situation?)   Yes   No   Transect ID: _____

Is the area a potential Problem Area?   Yes   No   Plot ID: *037*

VEGETATION

Dominant Plant Species	Stratum	Indicator	Dominant Plant Species	Stratum	Indicator
1. *FRPE*	T	*FACW*	9.		
2. *QULY*	T	*OBL*	10.		
3. *Hybiscus militaris*			11.		
4. *CEOC*	S	*OBL*	12.		
5. *Polygonum hydropiper*			13.		
6. *Forestiera*	S		14.		
7.			15.		
8.			16.		

Percent of Dominant Species that are OBL, FACW or FAC (excluding FACU): _____

Remarks:

HYDROLOGY

RECORDED DATA (Describe in Remarks):

☐ Stream, Lake, or Tide Gauge
☐ Aerial Photographs
☐ Other _____
☐ No Recorded Data Available

FIELD OBSERVATIONS:

Depth of Surface Water: _____ (in.)

Depth to Free Water in Pit: *8* (in.)

Depth to Saturated Soil: *burg.* (in.)

WETLAND HYDROLOGY INDICATORS:

Water in hole 8"

PRIMARY INDICATORS:

☒ Inundated
☒ Saturated in Upper 12 Inches
☒ Water Marks
☐ Drift Lines
☒ Sediment Deposits
☐ Drainage Patterns in Wetlands

SECONDARY INDICATORS (2 or more required):

☒ Oxidized Root Channels in Upper 12 Inches
☐ Water Stained Leaves
☐ Local Soil Survey Data
☐ FAC-Neutral Test
☐ Other (Explain in Remarks)

Environmental regulations specialists take detailed notes in the field—on everything from vegetation types to hydrology—and then use those notes in their work back in the office.

conduct environmental studies to determine company compliance with rules and regulations, and make recommendations to company leaders based on their findings. They might present these recommendations orally at a meeting, or they might compile them in a written report.

In some cases, an environmental regulations specialist will oversee a support staff. These individuals might assist the specialist by monitoring day-to-day concerns such as wastewater and chemical disposal or hazardous waste storage. They might conduct risk assessments or conduct research on endangered animal species inhabiting a proposed site for property development.

Necessary Skills

One of the key skills that all environmental regulations specialists have is a knack for details. When you're the one responsible for making sure your company follows the law, you don't want to miss anything. If you do, it could be a very expensive mistake.

Environmental regulations specialists are generally good communicators. Strong written and oral communication skills help environmental regulations specialists convey what they know to the people they're advising. The ability to use clear, concise language, especially when explaining complicated regulations that the average person might not understand, is critical.

If you become an environmental regulations specialist, chances are you'll be spending a good deal of time outdoors, "in the field." Toward that end, it helps to have a love for nature and to enjoy being outside in all kinds of weather.

The Environmental Protection Agency

It's important that environmental regulations specialists keep up with all of the latest federal environmental regulations passed by the U.S. Environmental Protection Agency (EPA). Established in 1970, the EPA is a government agency responsible for protecting the nation's environment. The EPA gives grants to environmental programs, organizations, institutions, and other entities. It also leads efforts to educate the public about the environment and maintains scientific research centers and laboratories. In addition, the EPA is responsible for writing the regulations for environmental laws passed by Congress. The EPA keeps a comprehensive list of all federal rules related to environmental protection on its Web site.

A Career as an Environmental Regulations Specialist

To become an environmental regulations specialist, you'll first need a four-year college degree. Having a BS or BA in natural science, urban planning, environmental studies, or even communications can help in this career. So can getting an internship at a company or government agency involved in environmental work. Beyond that, you could also pursue an advanced degree that would distinguish you from the competition, but it's probably not necessary— especially for your first job.

To land a senior position as an environmental regulations specialist, and one that potentially includes management responsibilities, you'd need many years of experience in

Environmental regulations specialists are often called upon to testify in court. Their testimony can be very valuable.

the environmental field. You'll also need experience in the industry for which you'll be working. For example, if you want a job at a nuclear energy company, it helps to have experience in the energy industry. Once you've proven your ability to oversee and delegate the work of others, handle large workloads, and get the job done smoothly and efficiently, you could apply for a management job. There are no specific certification or licensing requirements for environmental regulations specialists.

The Future of the Career

Environmental regulations specialists are paid based on their qualifications and experience. They're also paid according to the industry in which they work. An environmental regulations specialist at a major oil producer, for example, would likely be paid much more than one working for a local government agency devoted to municipal waste management. Private consultants who run their own firms make the highest salaries.

While there is no hard data on the career prospects for environmental regulations specialists, they are indispensable to any major company that creates waste in the manufacturing process, does business in environmentally sensitive areas, or does anything influenced by environmental law. Environmental regulations specialists should find no shortage of employment in the future, especially since so few people actually specialize in this line of work.

Glossary

administrative Having to do with management or supervising.

attorney A person who is authorized to practice law; a lawyer.

bar exam A state-administered exam that all law school graduates must pass before they are allowed to legally practice law in that state.

brief A document filed by an attorney prior to court that lists and explains all relevant facts and points of law applicable to that case.

client A person, business, or other entity that employs a lawyer or other legal professional for advice or representation.

cold-calling Calling people with whom one has had no prior contact in the hope of accomplishing one's objectives.

conservation The protection and preservation of natural resources and wildlife.

credentialed Having the proper qualifications to perform a job.

ecological Pertaining to the environment.

estuary An often ecologically diverse area where a river meets the ocean.

legal Having to do with the law.

legislator A lawmaker.

lobby To attempt to influence the decisions of politicians and lawmakers.

niche A particular area of specialization.

nonprofit A group or organization that does not exist to make a profit and that often receives outside support and funding for its operations.

private sector The private sector encompasses businesses, organizations, and entities that are not controlled by the government.

public sector Groups and other organizations that are run by the government are said to be in the public sector.

regulation A rule or law.

subpoena Also known as a summons, a subpoena is a document requiring that an individual appear in court.

wetlands Naturally wet lowland areas that are typically home to a wide variety of wildlife species.

For More Information

American Bar Association (ABA)
740 15th Street NW
Washington, DC 20005-1019
(202) 662-1000
Web site: http://www.abanet.org/environ
The ABA is the world's largest professional law
    association. If you become a lawyer, you'll probably
    join the ABA.

Canadian Environmental Law Association (CELA)
130 Spadina Avenue, Suite 301
Toronto, ON M5V 2L4
Canada
(416) 960-2284
Web site: http://www.cela.ca
CELA is a nonprofit public interest organization that uses
    law to protect the environment and fight for environ-
    mental law reforms.

Canadian Institute for Environmental Law
    and Policy (CIELAP)
130 Spadina Avenue, Suite 301
Toronto, ON M5V 2L4
Canada
(416) 923-5949
Web site: http://www.cielap.org
The research and educational branch of the Canadian
    Environmental Law Association, CIELAP uses research

findings to help develop laws and policies that protect the environment.

Center for International Environmental Law
1350 Connecticut Avenue NW, Suite 1100
Washington, DC 20036
(202) 785-8700
Web site: http://www.ciel.org
This nonprofit organization promotes ecological sustainability and works to solve environmental problems.

Earthjustice
426 17th Street, 6th Floor
Oakland, CA 94612-2820
(800) 584-6460
Web site: http://www.earthjustice.org
This nonprofit public interest law firm works to safeguard the environment.

Environmental Law Alliance Worldwide
1877 Garden Avenue
Eugene, OR 97403
(541) 687-8454
Web site: http://www.elaw.org
This international group helps public interest lawyers and scientists get the training they need.

Environmental Law Foundation
1736 Franklin Street, 9th Floor
Oakland, CA 94612
(510) 208-4555
Web site: http://www.envirolaw.org

The Environmental Law Foundation works to enforce
current environmental regulations and figures out
ways to address environmental problems.

Environmental Law Institute (ELI)
2000 L Street NW, Suite 620
Washington, DC 20036
(202) 939-3800
Web site: http://www.eli.org
ELI is a nonpartisan research and education center that
works to strengthen environmental protection through
improvements in law and governance worldwide.

National Association of Legal Assistants (NALA)
NALA Headquarters
1516 S. Boston, #200
Tulsa, OK 74119
(918) 587-6828
Web site: http://www.nala.org
This prominent nonprofit organization represents
thousands of paralegals and legal assistants in the
United States.

Web Sites

Due to the changing nature of Internet links, Rosen
Publishing has developed an online list of Web sites
related to the subject of this book. This site is updated
regularly. Please use this link to access the list:

http://www.rosenlinks.com/gca/law

For Further Reading

Brezina, Corona. *Careers in Law Enforcement*. New York, NY: Rosen Publishing, 2009.

Brezina, Corona. *Climate Change*. New York, NY: Rosen Publishing, 2008.

Daintith, John, and Jill Bailey, eds. *The Facts On File Dictionary of Ecology and the Environment*. New York, NY: Facts On File, 2003.

David, Sarah B. *Reducing Your Carbon Footprint at Home*. New York, NY: Rosen Publishing, 2009.

DeGalan, Julie, and Bryon Middlekauff. *Great Jobs for Environmental Studies Majors*. New York, NY: McGraw-Hill Companies, Inc., 2008.

Echaore-McDavid, Susan. *Career Opportunities in Law and the Legal Industry*. New York, NY: Checkmark Books, 2007.

Findley, Roger W., and Daniel A. Farber. *Environmental Law in a Nutshell*. St. Paul, MN: Thomson/West, 2008.

Greenland, Paul R., and Annamarie L. Sheldon. *Career Opportunities in Conservation and the Environment*. New York, NY: Checkmark Books, 2007.

Hunter, Malcolm L., David Lindenmayer, and Aram Calhoun. *Saving the Earth as a Career: Advice on Becoming a Conservation Professional*. Malden, MA: Blackwell Publishing, 2007.

Langholz, Jeffrey, Ph.D., and Kelly Turner. *You Can Prevent Global Warming (and Save Money!):*

51 Easy Ways. Kansas City, MO: Andrews McMeel Publishing, 2003.

Lazarus, Richard J., and Olivera A. Houck, eds. *Environmental Law Stories*. New York, NY: Foundation Press, 2005.

Miller, Louise. *Careers for Nature Lovers and Other Outdoor Types*. New York, NY: McGraw-Hill Companies, Inc., 2008.

Munneke, Gary. *Careers in Law*. New York, NY: McGraw-Hill Companies, Inc., 2004.

Nagle, Jeanne. *Living Green*. New York, NY: Rosen Publishing, 2003.

Salzman, James, and Barton H. Thompson Jr. *Environmental Law and Policy*. New York, NY: Foundation Press, 2007.

Schneider, Deborah, and Gary Belsky. *Should You Really Be a Lawyer? The Guide to Smart Career Choices Before, During, and After Law School*. Seattle, WA: LawyerAvenue Press, 2004.

Schneider, Steven. *The Everything Guide to Being a Paralegal: Winning Secrets to a Successful Career!* Avon, MA: Adams Media, 2006.

Bibliography

American League of Lobbyists. "Career Information."
    Retrieved April 10, 2009 (http://www.alldc.org/
    publicresources/career.cfm).
Bureau of Labor Statistics. *Occupational Outlook
    Handbook, 2008–09 Edition.* U.S. Department
    of Labor. Retrieved April 1, 2009 (http://www.
    bls.gov/oco).
Cohen, Adam. "With the Downturn, It's Time to Rethink
    the Legal Profession." *New York Times*, April 1, 2009.
    Retrieved April 1, 2009 (http://www.nytimes.com/
    2009/04/02/opinion/02thu4.html?scp=1&sq=
    rethink%20the%20legal%20profession&st=cse).
Commonwealth of Massachusetts. "Massachusetts
    Environmental Police." Retrieved April 7, 2009
    (http://www.mass.gov/dfwele/dle/welcome.htm).
League of Conservation Voters. "Re: Support H.R. 1, the
    American Recovery and Reinvestment Act of 2009."
    Retrieved April 10, 2009 (http://www.lcv.org/
    letter_hr1.pdf).
National Environmental Law Center. "Jobs with NELC."
    Retrieved April 14, 2009 (http://www.nelconline.org/
    nelc.asp?id2=8708#1).
National Federation of Paralegal Associations, Inc.
    "Paralegal Responsibilities." Retrieved April 2009
    (http://www.paralegals.org/associations/2270/
    files/Paralegal_Responsibilities.pdf).
National Federation of Paralegal Associations, Inc.
    "What Is a Paralegal?" Retrieved April 5, 2009

(http://www.paralegals.org/displaycommon.cfm?
an=1&subarticlenbr=110%20).

Navarro, Mireya. "Polluters, Beware: These Eco-Police
Officers Are for Real." *New York Times*, March 26,
2009. Retrieved April 7, 2009 (http://www.nytimes.
com/2009/03/26/nyregion/26ecocops.html?
ref=todayspaper).

New York State Department of Environmental
Conservation. "Environmental Conservation Police
Officers." Retrieved April 7, 2009 (http://www.
dec.ny.gov/regulations/2437.html).

New York State Department of Environmental
Conservation. "Newest Class of ECOs, Forest
Rangers, and Park Police Graduate." Retrieved April 7,
2009 (http://www.dec.ny.gov/press/12510.html).

North American Wildlife Enforcement Officers
Association. "NAWEOA FAQs." Retrieved April 7,
2009 (http://www.naweoa.org/become-a-wco.htm).

Oklahoma Energy Resources Board. "Environmental/
Regulatory Specialist." Retrieved April 11, 2009
(http://www.oerb.com/Default.aspx?tabid=74).

Paul L. Boley Law Library. "Careers in Environmental Law."
Lewis & Clark Law School Podcasts, September 27,
2007. Retrieved April 14, 2009 (http://lawlib.lclark.
edu/podcast/?p=321).

Rhode Island Environmental Police. "Class Title:
Environmental Police Officer I." Retrieved April 7,
2009 (http://www.dem.ri.gov/programs/bnatres/
enforce/pdfs/jobdesc.pdf).

State of Rhode Island, Department of Environmental
Management, Division of Law Enforcement. "How to
Become an Environmental Police Officer." Retrieved

April 7, 2009 (http://www.dem.ri.gov/programs/
bnatres/enforce/epojob.htm).

SustainLane. "Administrative Assistant or Legal
Secretary: Lawyers for Clean Water, Inc."
Retrieved April 11, 2009 (http://www.sustainlane.
com/jobs/administrative-assistant-or-legal-
secretary-lawyers-for-clean-water-inc/
73O7XT7SLONAQID4CLSUNLI8YBC8).

University of Cincinnati. "U.S. Department of Justice
2009 Honors Paralegal Intern Program." College of
Education, Criminal Justice, and Human Services.
Retrieved April 5, 2009 (http://www.ups.edu/
Documents/CES/ParalegalInternProgram.pdf).

University of East London. "Job Profile: Lobbyist." Retrieved
April 10, 2009 (http://www.environmentalcareers.
org.uk/careers/job/lobbyist.asp).

Washington Environmental Council. "What We Do:
Engage Decision Makers." Retrieved April 10,
2009 (http://www.wecprotects.org/what-we-do/
engage-decision-makers).

Water Environment Federation. "Environmental Specialist."
Retrieved April 11, 2009 (http://www.wef.org/
MembershipCareers/JobResources/CareerPaths/
Environmental+Specialist.htm).

Index

About the Author

Chris Hayhurst is a writer and editor living in southern New Hampshire. He has written on numerous subjects for Rosen Publishing, including the human brain, genetics, and sports.

Photo Credits

Cover Tim Sloan/AFP/Getty Images; pp. 1 (left), 36 Emmanuel/AFP/Getty Images; p. 1 (right) © www.istockphoto.com/paul kline; pp. 4–5 © www.istockphoto.com/Frances Twitty; pp. 7, 11, 13, 44, 47, 49, 51, 55, 57, 59, 61, 63 © AP Images; p. 17 © Jim West/The Image Works; p. 19 © Dan Honda/Contra Costa Times/ZUMA Press; p. 23 krtphotoslive/Newscom.com; p. 25 © Syracuse Newspapers/David Lassman/The Image Works; p. 28 © www.istockphoto.com/Sandra O'Claire; p. 30 © www.istockphoto.com/Brent Holland; p. 33 © www.istockphoto.com/David Lewis; p. 34 © www.istockphoto.com/Markanja; p. 39 Ohio Department of Natural Resources; p. 43 © Cydney Scott/Palm Beach Post/ZUMA Press; p. 66 Michael Bryant/Philadelphia Inquirer/Newscom.com.

Designer: Sam Zavieh; Photo Researcher: Amy Feinberg